MODERN ROLE MODELS

Michael Jordan

Judy Hasday

Mason Crest Publishers

Produced by OTTN Publishing in association with
21st Century Publishing and Communications, Inc.

MASON CREST PUBLISHERS INC.
370 Reed Road
Broomall, Pennsylvania 19008
(866) MCP-BOOK (toll free)
www.masoncrest.com

Printed in the United States of America.

First Printing

9 8 7 6 5 4 3 2 1

Library of Congress Cataloging-in-Publication Data

Hasday, Judy L., 1957–
    Michael Jordan / Judy Hasday.
        p. cm. — (Modern role models)
    Includes bibliographical references and index.
    ISBN 978-1-4222-0483-2 (hardcover) — ISBN 978-1-4222-0771-0 (pbk.)
    1. Jordan, Michael, 1963–   —Juvenile literature. 2. Basketball players—United
States—Biography—Juvenile literature. I. Title.
GV884.J67H37 2008
796.323092—dc22
[B]   2008025304

Publisher's note:
All quotations in this book come from original sources, and contain the spelling
and grammatical inconsistencies of the original text.

CROSS-CURRENTS

*In the ebb and flow of the currents of life we are each influenced
by many people, places, and events that we directly experience
or have learned about. Throughout the chapters of this book you
will come across CROSS-CURRENTS reference boxes. These
boxes direct you to a CROSS-CURRENTS section in the back
of the book that contains fascinating and informative sidebars
and related pictures. Go on. ▶▶*

CONTENTS

Wearing his famous number 23, Chicago Bulls guard Michael Jordan shoots a jumper over Utah Jazz guard Jeff Hornacek. At game six of the 1998 NBA finals, held in the Delta Center, in Salt Lake City, the contest between the Bulls of the Eastern Conference and the Jazz of the Western Conference would come down to the final seconds.

With 5.2 Seconds Left

CHICAGO BULLS COCAPTAIN MICHAEL JORDAN HAD already helped his team earn five National Basketball Association (NBA) championships as of June 14, 1998. The 6'6" guard, who was regarded as the best to ever play the game of basketball, was eager to help his team bring home another championship title.

At the 1998 NBA Finals Michael's team was looking to win its third championship title in a row for a second time by defeating the Utah Jazz that June night. Jordan and the Chicago Bulls were just one game away from repeating their "**three-peat**."

⇛ DEFYING THE ODDS ⇚

At the beginning of the 1997-98 season, not many Chicago Bulls fans thought their team would make it to the NBA finals the following

June. They complained that there was no cohesiveness among the players. Bulls cocaptain Scottie Pippen was injured, and he ended up missing the first 35 games of the season. Flamboyant **rebound** king Dennis Rodman seemed distracted by his own celebrity, often showing up to games with his hair dyed different colors. Before the start of the 1997-1998 NBA season, Jordan's own presence on the team had been uncertain. He would later write in his autobiography *For the Love of the Game*:

> **The Bulls knew I wouldn't come back and play for anyone but [coach] Phil [Jackson]. After the 1997 championship, they knew they had to sign Phil before they went after me. But they put a clause in Phil's contract that said if I didn't sign by a certain date Phil's deal was void.**

Jordan ended up signing a one-year contract in time to ensure that Phil Jackson would guide the Bulls through one more season as coach. Team fans speculated that this was probably the last year all of the key Chicago Bulls players would be together. Bulls' owner Jerry Reinsdorf and his general manager Jerry Krause had asserted they could no longer afford to keep the team together. Reinsdorf said he knew at some point down the road he was going to regret agreeing to pay Jordan market value. That comment soured Jordan on his boss, he later wrote in his book:

> **After all these years, after all these championships, after all I had tried to do for the Bulls organization, after all those years of being underpaid and you regret paying me market value? It was like a punch in the heart.**

⟫ INTO THE PLAYOFFS ⟪

However, despite the behind-the-scenes discontent, the team played well. The Bulls finished the regular season with 62 wins and 20 losses. Because the Bulls had the best record in the Eastern Conference, they had the home court advantage through the first three rounds of the **playoffs**. The Bulls beat the New Jersey Nets (3-0), the Charlotte Hornets (4-1), and the Indiana Pacers (4-3).

Michael Jordan (center) with teammates Scottie Pippen (right) and Dennis Rodman. A versatile forward who could deliver powerful defense and offense, Pippen joined the Chicago Bulls in 1987. Rodman, renowned for his relentless rebounding abilities, joined the Bulls as a forward in 1995. The three players were key to the success of the Chicago Bulls during the 1990s.

During the 1990s Michael Jordan led the Chicago Bulls to six NBA championships in eight years. In this June 16, 1998, photograph, Jordan holds up six fingers to show how many NBA titles the Bulls have as he addresses fans in Chicago's Grant Park celebrating the most recent win.

Michael Jordan and Scottie Pippen were the one-two punch of the Chicago Bulls offense. The Utah Jazz had their equivalent in seasoned players Karl Malone and John Stockton. The Bulls had played the Jazz for the NBA championship title the season before, and the Utah team had been formidable. In the end, however, the Bulls had won the 1997 series in six games. The 1998 NBA finals promised to be just as exciting and challenging.

⇒ LAST TIME FOR #23 ⇐

The series lived up to its hype. After five games, Chicago had the edge, leading the series 3-2. All of the games in the Final had been close, with all but one going down to the final minute of play. For most of game six, the score remained close. With less than a minute left, John Stockton sank a three-pointer to give Utah an 86-83 lead, sending the sold-out hometown crowd into a frenzy.

The Utah players knew Michael Jordan was the Bulls' unstoppable guy. And the more pressure-packed the situation, the better Jordan played. When Chicago called time-out with 41 seconds left on the game clock, the strategy in the huddle was simple: Get the ball to number 23—Michael Jordan.

Scottie Pippen threw the inbounds pass to Jordan. He circled to his right, before surging towards the basket and leaping over Utah forward Antoine Carr. With 37 seconds left Jordan shoveled a layup off the backboard glass and into the net, cutting Utah's lead to one. Still leading by a single point, the Jazz had possession as Stockton took the ball, dribbled it down the court, and passed it to Malone. But then Jordan moved in and slapped the ball away from Malone with 18 seconds left. Without pausing, Jordan and the Bulls headed up the court for one last shot. Jordan described those last seconds:

> **"It was like I was watching everything unfold in slow motion on television. I stole the ball, looked up at the clock, and then down the court. I could see every player and I remember exactly where they were as I came up the floor."**

All of this happened within about 11 seconds. Jordan, covered by Byron Russell, started to charge to the basket, but then suddenly pulled up, causing Russell to slip to the floor. In that instant, Jordan put up a 20-foot jump shot, hitting nothing but net. With 5.2 seconds left, Chicago led the game 87-86. One last shot by Utah failed, and Michael Jordan and the Bulls were the 1998 NBA champions. For the sixth time in his career Jordan was named **MVP** of the playoff series. Amid all the celebrating, few people knew that Jordan's game-winning shot would be his last as a Chicago Bull.

CROSS-CURRENTS

To learn about other championship series most valuable players, read "Notable MVPs in NBA Finals History." Go to page 47. ▶▶

A young Michael Jordan poses in his baseball uniform. He has said that as a kid he loved to play sports and "wasn't really a work conscious type of person." As a result, his parents thought that of all the kids in the family, he was the least likely to succeed. That attitude made Michael work hard to prove his parents wrong.

From "Least Likely" to Superstar

MICHAEL JEFFREY JORDAN WAS BORN ON FEBRU-
ary 17, 1963. His father, James, worked as a forklift
operator for the General Electric Company (GE) and his
mother, Deloris, was a full-time homemaker when the
children were small. Michael had three older siblings:
James, Larry, and Deloris, and a younger sister Roslyn.

When Michael was an infant, the Jordan family lived in Brooklyn,
New York, while his father attended a GE training school. The family
then moved back to James's hometown of Wallace, North Carolina, a
small town located in the eastern part of the state, about 25 miles
away from the Atlantic coastline.

In 1970, when Michael was 7 years old, the Jordan family moved to
Wilmington, North Carolina. There, the young boy often participated

in a variety of sports. He was a good baseball player. As a teenager, Michael helped his team win the Babe Ruth League state championship. In one interview, he shared how he felt about the triumph of not only winning the game with his team but also earning special recognition. He said:

> **My favorite childhood memory, my greatest accomplishment was when I got the [Babe Ruth League] Most Valuable Player award. . . . This was the first big thing I accomplished and you always remember the first.**

THE COMPETITOR

In speaking about her five children, Deloris would later recall that Michael was very competitive, even as a kid. And he often preferred to compete against the older kids:

> **He always, I think was a little bit above his level. Very competitive. They all had their own goals and things they wanted to achieve. But Michael always wanted to be with the big boys.**

The three brothers would often play for hours where the basketball hoop was set up in the backyard.

The feeling of being in competition with his brothers carried over to Michael comparing himself unfavorably with his more academically oriented younger sister, Roslyn. In addition, Michael sometimes got into trouble at school, cutting classes to practice basketball or getting into an altercation with another student over name-calling. Years later, Michael would tell an interviewer that based on his behavior as a youth, he would have probably been the "least likely to succeed" in his class.

BASKETBALL WAS "IT"

At age 14, Michael had enrolled at Emsley A. Laney High School, in Wilmington, North Carolina, where he competed in baseball, football, and basketball. In his sophomore year, he tried out for but didn't make the varsity basketball team. Michael was devastated, he would later tell an interviewer:

Michael displays his high-flying moves during a Laney High School basketball game. When he didn't make the varsity team his sophomore year, Jordan stepped up his basketball workouts and earned a spot on the team as a junior. His performance on the court during the last two years of high school earned him a scholarship from the University of North Carolina.

> ❝It was embarrassing not making that team. They posted the roster and it was there for a long, long time without my name on it. I remember being really mad, too, because there was a guy who made it that really wasn't as good as me.❞

Determined to play varsity basketball for his high school, Michael worked out and trained hard. That summer, he also grew another four inches, going from 5'11" to 6'3". The hard work paid off. His junior year, he made the Laney High School team. He requested his now-famous jersey number 23 because it was roughly half the number 45, which had been his brother Larry's jersey number.

Michael attended many basketball clinics while in high school. One of them was run by University of North Carolina (UNC) coach Dean Smith. He noticed the young basketball player's acrobatic skills in dunking and layups. Although college recruiting scouts also took notice of Michael Jordan, in the fall of 1981 he decided to be one of the entering freshmen at UNC.

CROSS-CURRENTS

Coach Dean Smith coached the Tar Heels for more than 35 years. To learn more about him, read "Dean Smith, UNC Men's Basketball Coach." Go to page 48. ▶▶

⟫ FIRST YEAR TAR HEEL ⟪

During Michael's freshman year as a UNC Tar Heel, he was named to the starting lineup. There, he joined teammates James Worthy and Sam Perkins—two players who would go on to have successful NBA careers in their own right. Once Michael got over his initial nervousness, he settled in and flourished as a player.

As the university basketball season progressed, Michael evolved into a great player. In only his third game of the season, he scored 22 points, made four **steals**, and blocked a shot against the ninth-ranked Tulsa Golden Hurricanes to help UNC win the game 78-70.

Michael was also getting attention for his superb play. Compliments on his abilities came from teammates and sportswriters in the local papers. UNC point guard Jimmy Black was quoted as saying that Michael could do it all—score, defend, block shots, rebound, and even "quarterback" the team.

The Tar Heels and their **rookie** star had an amazing season, going 12-2 in the season. In March 1982 the UNC team made it to the National Collegiate Athletic Association (**NCAA**) championship final,

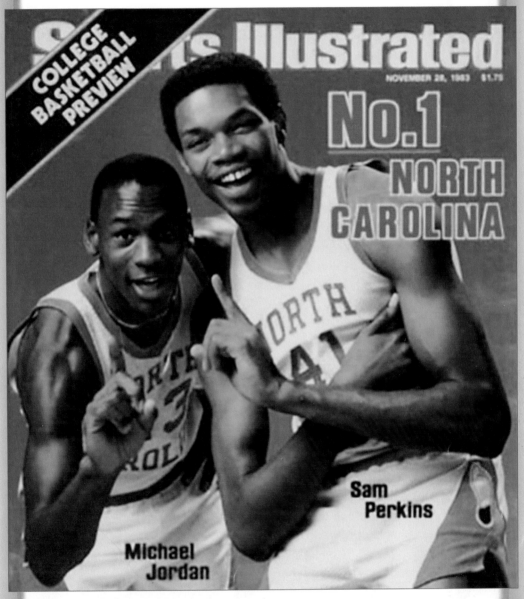

Michael Jordan and Sam Perkins appear on the cover of the November 28, 1983, *Sports Illustrated* magazine. Both North Carolina University players would go on to play for the national men's basketball team at the 1984 Olympics and have stellar NBA careers. In his three seasons playing for UNC, Jordan averaged 17.7 points and 5.0 rebounds per game.

where the Tar Heels defeated the Georgetown Hoyas 63-62. Michael hit the winning jump shot to clinch the championship and give Coach Dean Smith his first NCAA title.

⇛ ON THE RISE ⇚

Over the next few years Michael continued to elevate his own play, but the Tar Heels were not the same power force team without Worthy, who entered the 1982 NBA **draft** and was picked by the Los Angeles Lakers. In his sophomore year Michael earned College Player of the Year honors, and even though he never again played in an NCAA Final, he never stopped wanting to be a better basketball player, continuing to focus on improving his game through hours and hours of practice and pick-up games.

The summer following his sophomore year, Michael traveled with a team of college all-stars to Caracas, Venezuela, where they

Michael talks to reporters about being a UNC Tar Heel while his proud parents, Deloris and James Jordan, look on. Michael says his parents were hardworking, generous, and disciplined with him and his siblings when they were growing up. He has often said they were his biggest role models.

represented the United States in the Pan American Games. The USA basketball team won the gold medal, with Michael leading the team in scoring. He enjoyed the international experience so much he finally settled on cultural geography as his major at UNC.

During Michael's junior year on the court, his game was off. People wondered if all the attention he was getting was causing too much pressure on the 20-year-old athlete. Michael's father gave his own view, telling his son that he was trying too hard, and he just needed to be Michael and play his game. From that point on, Michael played again like the gifted college ball player he had always been.

UNC made it to the 1984 NCAA Tournament, but lost in the second round to the Indiana Hoosiers. Michael decided that there was really nothing more he could accomplish in the college ranks. At the end of his junior year, he made the difficult decision to leave school and turn pro. In the NBA draft, Michael was selected third overall. His new team was the Chicago Bulls.

CROSS-CURRENTS

To learn more about other people who gained fame after attending the University of North Carolina, read "Notable UNC Alumni." Go to page 49. ▶▶

⟫ INTERNATIONAL SPOTLIGHT ⟪

Before Michael started his rookie season with the Bulls, he had one more amateur challenge left—the 1984 summer Olympics in Los Angeles, California. In addition to Michael, the US team included future NBA stars Chris Mullin, Patrick Ewing, and Sam Perkins. In the medal rounds the men's national basketball team, coached by Bobby Knight, eliminated the teams from China, Canada, and Uruguay before meeting Spain in the finals.

In an awesome display of athleticism, Michael scored a team-high 20 points, helping the United States achieve a 96-65 win—and the Olympic gold medal. His international exposure catapulted him into instant fame.

With the games over, Michael headed to Chicago to begin his NBA career with a team that was without a true leader on the court. He was going to a city that was as hungry for success as he was. And he had made an endorsement deal with a little-known company that made sneakers. The sneaker company was named Nike and its designers were going to create a signature sneaker just for Michael—the Air Jordan. The shoe and the nickname would become NBA legend.

MICHAEL JORDAN
BULLS • GUARD-FORWARD

Jordan's rookie year trading card. Michael was selected third overall in the NBA draft by the Chicago Bulls, behind Hakeem Olajuwon and Sam Bowie. In May 1985, with an average of 28.2 points and having played in all 82 games of the season, he would be named NBA Rookie of the Year.

3

Three-Peat

MICHAEL JORDAN WAS JOINING A TEAM IN NEED of a leader. The Chicago Bulls had begun to play in the NBA league in 1966. Initially, the team did well, making it to the playoffs in its first year. By the 1970s and 80s, however, fans did not have much to cheer about. In 1983 the Bulls had posted a dismal 27-55 record.

The addition of Michael Jordan to the roster in the summer of 1984 was an exciting prospect for a city desperate for a winner. No one expected the team to win a championship in Michael's first season, but fans and management hoped his coming to Chicago would make for exciting basketball.

⇒ ROOKIE SEASON ⇐

In his rookie season (1984-85) with the Chicago Bulls, Michael gave fans at home and on the road plenty of thrilling basketball to watch. He was a scoring machine, pumping in points per game in the 30 to

40 range. His presence on the team attracted numerous fans. Average attendance for the Chicago **franchise** went from 6,365 a game the year before Michael joined the team to 11,887.

Celtics great Larry Bird had been amazed by Michael's talent. After one game between the Bulls and Celtics, Bird told a sportswriter:

> **"Even at this stage of his career he's doing more than I ever did. I couldn't do what he does as a rookie. . . . [T]here was one drive tonight: He had the ball up in his right hand, then he took it down, then he brought it back up. I got a hand on it, fouled him, and he still scored. All the while he's in the air."**

In February 1985 Michael was voted to the Eastern Conference team for the NBA **All-Star Game**. At the end of the season, in May, he was named NBA Rookie of the Year.

CROSS-CURRENTS

For more information about past award-winning NBA rookie players, read "NBA Rookies of the Year." Go to page 50. ▶▶

⇒ UNEXPECTED TIME OFF ⇐

Despite his great rookie season, Michael received criticisms. Some people complained that he was doing all the scoring and not playing "team" basketball.

The following season, Michael did not have to worry about how he was being perceived. A broken foot suffered during a game against the Golden State Warriors early in the 1985-86 season kept him on the bench. Michael used the time off to complete his academic work at UNC and earn his college degree.

⇒ THINGS COMING TOGETHER ⇐

With his foot healed, Michael came back strong in the 1986-87 season. Although the Bulls had another losing season (40-42), they still made the playoffs. In the first round, they lost to the Boston Celtics. Michael scored an NBA record of 63 points in game two.

It was clear that the team was in need of players who would complement Michael's abilities and provide consistent scoring and defensive play. By the following season, the Bulls top brass had found those players. Horace Grant came through the 1987 NBA draft and the Bulls acquired Scottie Pippen from the Seattle Supersonics. With John Paxon, Grant, and Pippen in the lineup, the Bulls went 50-32 for

Michael goes up in the air for a dunk while Magic Johnson of the Los Angeles Lakers looks on during a 1986 game in Los Angeles, California. Jordan's remarkable leaping ability made him appear to fly on the court, a talent that earned him nicknames like "Air Jordan" and "His Airness," in addition to being known simply as M. J.

the season and made it to the second round of the NBA playoffs before losing to the Detroit Pistons.

Over the next two years the Bulls continued to strengthen their lineup. The team acquired center Bill Cartwright, and Pippen and Grant came into their own as premiere NBA players. In addition, a major team change occurred during the 1989-90 season when assistant coach Phil Jackson replaced Doug Collins as head coach. Jackson would bring a new approach to coaching that would help the Chicago Bulls dominate the next decade.

⇒ A NEW LIFE ⇐

Michael had become a player of superstar status. For four years in a row, he was the league's leading scorer. Fan attendance to Bulls home games was at an all-time high and his Nike endorsement deals were worth over $20 million. In 1989 he signed a new eight-year contract with the team that was worth $25 million.

His personal life was changing too. He had met a young woman named Juanita Vanoy. The two fell in love, and in September 1989 they married.

Wanting to give back to the community, Michael established the Michael Jordan Foundation that year. His charity supported educational organizations such as the United Negro College Fund, and it helped sick and handicapped children through the Make-a-Wish Foundation.

⇒ MOTIVATED TO WIN ⇐

The Bulls had been getting close to winning an NBA championship but had not been able to get past the Detroit Pistons in their three post-season match-ups. In Phil Jackson's first year as head coach, the Bulls finished the 1989-90 season 55-27. The Chicago team then breezed through the first and second round of the playoffs before falling short once more against the Pistons in a grueling seven-game series. The Pistons went on to win the NBA championship against the Portland Trail Blazers.

That loss made Michael determined to see the Bulls achieve their first NBA championship. During the 1990-91 season, he was phenomenal: Michael scored his 15,000th career point, was named to the All-Star team for the seventh year, and averaged 31.5 points per game.

Jordan (center) makes a high-flying, tongue-wagging dunk in this photograph from a 1989 game against the Cleveland Cavaliers. He would say that the habit of sticking out his tongue while making a shot came from his father, James, who would do the same thing while concentrating on his work.

The Bulls finished the season 61-21 and for the seventh straight year reached the playoffs. The Chicago team blew through the playoff games, winning eleven (including a 4-0 rout of their arch-rival Pistons) and losing only one. While the playoffs were taking place, Michael received the NBA most valuable player award for the 1990-91 season. But he told reporters at the news conference there was an award he would much rather earn, saying:

> **"I'm envious of the Detroit Pistons, the Los Angeles Lakers, the Boston Celtics: the teams that have celebrated winning championships. That's something I badly want to taste. It's the driving force for me right now.**
>
> **Winning the M.V.P. award is great, and I graciously accept it on behalf of my family, my teammates and the Chicago Bulls organization. But I'd much rather be standing here in June, waiting to receive a championship ring."**

➤ CHAMPIONS ◄

In the finals, the Bulls faced a formidable opponent—the Los Angeles Lakers—whose players included Magic Johnson and Michael's former UNC teammates James Worthy and Sam Perkins. After losing the first game at home, the Bulls went on to sweep the next four games and win the 1991 NBA championship.

In the locker room, Michael wept openly as he hugged the NBA championship trophy. He told reporters it was the proudest day of his life—a moment no one could ever take away from him. The city of Chicago threw a huge celebratory parade honoring the Bulls. More than 500,000 fans met the team at a rally at Grant Park. When Michael spoke to the crowd, he recalled the seven-year struggle of going from the bottom of the league to the top. Through hard work and perseverance, the Bulls gave Chicago its first NBA championship.

It is not unusual for a team to repeat a championship performance in sports. The following season the Bulls played like champions. Finishing the 1991-92 season with an incredible 67-15 record, ten games better than their closest competitor, the Bulls were ready to defend their title in the playoffs. And they prevailed, beating the Cleveland Cavaliers 4-2 to earn a return trip to the NBA finals. The

Michael hugs the championship trophy after the Chicago Bulls defeated the Lakers in game five of the NBA finals, held June 12, 1991, in Los Angles, California. The title was the first NBA championship for the Bulls, who won the series, 4-1. M. J. was named the NBA Finals Most Valuable Player—the first of six NBA Finals MVP awards.

final series against the Portland Trail Blazers went six games, with the Bulls coming out victorious. The Chicago Bulls had their second championship in as many years.

During the summer of 1992, Michael joined other NBA superstars to form the U.S. men's basketball **Dream Team**. It was Jordan's second trip to the Olympics, which were held in Barcelona, Spain. Once again, the men's national team came home with a gold medal. Jordan was the only Dream Team member to start every game, and he was the team's top scorer.

When the Dream Team returned from Barcelona, Michael switched his focus back to NBA basketball. His team had won two championships in a row, and he was looking for a third. Only two teams, the Minnesota Lakers (1951-54) and the Boston Celtics (1958-1966) had won at least three straight championships.

The Bulls ended the regular 1992-93 season 57-25, finishing first in the Central Division. They made it into the playoffs easily, and closed out their first two rounds undefeated against the Atlanta Hawks and Cleveland Cavaliers. It took six games to beat the New York Knicks to make a third trip to the finals.

Michael Jordan in action against Mark West of the Phoenix Suns in game four of the 1993 NBA finals, held on June 16 at the Chicago Stadium. The Bulls won the game and went on to win the series 4-2, clinching a "three-peat." Jordan averaged 41 points during the series—an NBA finals record.

The only thing left standing in the way of a Bulls' three-peat was the team from Arizona—the Phoenix Suns. They had finished the regular season with the best record in the NBA. Playing against stars like Charles Barkley, Kevin Johnson, and Dan Majerle only added to Michael's motivation to win. In another exciting finals series, the Bulls would not be denied. They won the series 4-2. For the third time Michael was named the NBA Finals MVP.

⟫ TRAGEDY AND ENDINGS ⟪

After the hoopla of celebrating the Bulls' three-peat, Michael looked forward to a summer of relaxing and playing golf—his other "favorite" sport. But then tragedy struck. On July 22, Michael's 56-year-old father, James, attended a family friend's funeral in North Carolina. On his return trip home, driving the new car his son had given him, he disappeared. Three weeks later, law enforcement authorities delivered tragic news to the Jordan family. James Jordan's body had been found floating in a creek in South Carolina. He had been shot and killed during a robbery while he slept in his car at a rest stop in North Carolina.

James had been Michael's best friend and one of his biggest supporters. The murder came as terrible shock to him and his family. They released a prepared statement:

> **“Dad is no longer with us. But the lessons he taught us will give us strength to move forward with a renewed sense of purpose in our lives.”**

James Jordan's sudden senseless death led Michael to reevaluate his own life. During the 1992-93 season, he had already been weighing retirement from the game. At a press conference on October 6, 1993, Michael told reporters that he felt that basketball had no challenges for him anymore. His father's death made him realize life was short, and he now wanted to spend more time with his family. With his wife, Juanita, at his side, he announced his retirement. One of the NBA's' greatest players was leaving the game, ending an exciting era in pro basketball.

Pro basketball superstar Michael Jordan in a Hanes ad. During the 1990s Jordan became one of the highest-paid athletes in the history of team sports due to his many endorsements deals. Michael's longtime association with Nike had begun in 1984—before he even played in the NBA—when the sports apparel company gave him a half-million deal and signature shoe line.

"I'm Back"

BY THE FALL OF 1993, MICHAEL JORDAN HAD accomplished a great deal. In professional basketball, he had set and broken records in almost every area of the game. He had proven himself as one of the most successful pro athletes. Numerous endorsements with companies like Nike, Gatorade, and Hanes earned him millions of dollars each year.

In the beginning of his retirement, Michael talked about how he enjoyed taking his three children, Jeffrey, Marcus, and Jasmine, to school. He played golf. He attended the opening game of the Bulls 1993-94 season and the accompanying ceremony commemorating the team's third NBA championship. At the event, Michael received his third NBA championship ring. Then for the first time in his life, he sat as a spectator and watched the Bulls play.

⇒ PLAYING HARDBALL ⇐

But Michael had other plans, as he has explained in later interviews. After the first Bulls' championship in 1991, he says, he had been thinking about leaving basketball to play professional baseball. He and his father had often talked about Michael making a try at baseball after he felt he had done all he could in basketball.

Chicago Bulls' owner Jerry Reinsdorf also owned the Chicago White Sox, a Major League Baseball (MLB) team. Michael asked Reinsdorf for permission to work out with the White Sox, explaining that he wanted to see if he had the skills necessary to play major league ball competitively. In January 1994, Michael made the move to baseball official. He announced that he was going to sign a contract with the Chicago White Sox.

There have been other pro athletes who have played in more than one sport successfully, but none have stopped playing for several years before going back to their first sport. Michael needed to determine whether he had the physical skills and the mental determination required of a MLB player. His defensive play and his base-running abilities were never in question. But his ability to hit well and with consistency were unknown.

CROSS-CURRENTS

For information about other professional sports figures who have showed their athletic prowess in additional fields, read "Pro Athletes Who Play Other Sports." Go to page 50. ▶▶

It soon became apparent that Michael needed time to get his playing skills up to major league ability. He was sent to the White Sox minor league AA farm team, the Birmingham Barons. Although it took Michael seven at-bats to get his first hit, he was not discouraged. In fact, he was humbled, but not defeated. In April 1994 he told the *New York Times*:

> **❝For the last nine years, I lived in a situation where I had the world at my feet. Now I'm just another minor leaguer in the clubhouse here trying to make it to the major leagues.❞**

⟫ MLB STRIKE ⟪

Michael never had the chance to improve over time. He intended to return to playing baseball for a second season in 1995. But the previous fall, Major League Baseball players went on strike. When it was time to report for spring training in February 1995, the strike still hadn't been settled. Michael had been given the chance to move

After working out with the Chicago White Sox during spring training in February 1994, Michael was assigned to the minor league team, the Birmingham Barons the following April. He continued to play in the minor leagues that September, when he joined the Scottsdale Scorpions in the Arizona Fall league. In this photograph he wears the Scorpion uniform while at batting practice.

up to the majors, but to do so meant defying the strike. His decision to honor the strike meant his baseball career was over.

CROSS-CURRENTS

For more details about Michael's attempt to excel in another sport, read "Jordan's Brief Baseball Career." Go to page 52. ▶▶

On April 2, 1995, the MLB strike ended. But by then Michael had returned to the Chicago Bulls. He decided to come out of retirement, announcing his return on March 18, 1995, with a press release. It contained two simple words: "I'm back."

⟩⟩ BACK IN BUSINESS ⟨⟨

After Michael's first game back with the Chicago Bulls on March 19, he told reporters that despite his mediocre performance that night, he realized that he loved the game too much to stay away. He was happy to be back—in the game, with his teammates, and playing in front of basketball fans around the country.

Everywhere Michael went he was greeted by standing ovations amid thunderous applause. At the end of the regular season, the Bulls made it to the playoffs. However, they lost in the second round to the Orlando Magic.

During the off season Michael was approached to do a live-action/animated movie in which he would star opposite the animated character Bugs Bunny and other Warner Brothers Looney Tunes characters. Concerned that he was not in top conditioning for playing basketball, Michael agreed to do the movie only if he could continue his workout training. The details were worked out and a state-of-the-art gymnasium was built for Michael to use during filming. He had plenty of company for pick-up games as many NBA players showed up to play basketball on Michael's court. The movie, named *Space Jam*, was later released in November 1996.

At the start of the 1995-96 NBA season, Michael was determined to get himself and the Bulls another shot at the championship. The Bulls started out 12-2 for the month of November.

During the run, Michael took time out to attend the opening of the James R. Jordan Boys and Girls Club and Family Life Center, which serves the residents of Chicago's West Side. Built in memory of Michael's father, the Center serves more than 1,000 inner-city kids and their families each week. They can take classes ranging from courses in computer skills, pottery, cooking classes, and photography.

Basketball star Michael Jordan poses with a Bugs Bunny mockup at a November 1996 news conference announcing the release of *Space Jam*—a live-action and animated film by Warner Brothers. During the eight weeks of filming in Burbank, California, in 1995 he and other NBA players made use of a temporary workout facility referred to as "The Jordan Dome."

Michael makes a layup shot against the New York Knicks in game five of the Eastern Conference semifinals during the 1996 NBA playoffs at the May 14, 1996, game in Chicago. During the 1995-96 regular season, the Bulls had a record 72 wins. The following June the team would go on to earn its fourth NBA championship title.

⇒ BACK ON TOP ⇐

The Bulls finished the 1995-96 season with an astounding 72-10 record. It was the team's and coach Phil Jackson's winningest season ever, and the best record in NBA history. The Bulls continued their winning streak during the NBA playoffs, finishing off the Knicks 4-1, defeating the Orlando Magic 4-0, and taking a commanding 3-0 lead against the Seattle Supersonics in the finals.

Bu then the Bulls lost two games in a row. The teams next met on Sunday, June 16—Father's Day. Michael would later tell interviewers that it was difficult to play that day. The Bulls were on the brink of capturing a fourth NBA title, and if they did, it would be the first time James would not be there to celebrate with Michael. The Sonics played tough, but in the end the Bulls won the game 87-75.

On their home court, the Bulls fans went wild. Michael's teammates celebrated on the court with Scottie Pippen, Dennis Rodman, Toni Kukoc, and others high-fiving and embracing one another. But Michael had grabbed the game ball and lay facedown on the court, holding on to the ball as tears flowed freely down his face. All of the emotions he bottled up during the game suddenly overtook the four-time champion.

Michael would later explain that he had felt compelled to win another championship to gain credibility for his return to the game. He was overcome by the realization that he had accomplished what he set out to do. And he was grieving because for the first time in his career, he could not share his latest achievement with his father.

⇒ THE STRIVE FOR FIVE ⇐

Coming off the emotional upheaval of the 1996 championship, the Bulls set their sights the following season on defending their NBA title. Some quietly asked if it was possible for the Bulls to repeat their amazing feat from 1991, 1992, and 1993. Words like *dynasty* were being used to describe the Chicago Bulls of the 1990s, and with good reason. By the All-Star break in February 1997, they were 42-6.

Michael, playing in his 11th All-Star Game scored 14 points, while pulling down 11 rebounds and making 11 **assists**. It was the first time in the NBA event that a player achieved the **triple-double**.

At the end of the 1996-97 season, the Bulls had the best record in the league—69 wins and 13 losses. They entered the playoffs in a game against the Washington Bullets on April 25, 1997. After sweeping the series four straight, they lost only two games out of their next eight to reach the NBA finals against the Utah Jazz. The teams split the first four games with the crucial game five played in Utah. Despite coming down with the flu, Michael played in the game. He scored 38 points to lift the Bulls to a 3-2 lead in the series.

The sixth game got off to a slow start before the Jazz went ahead by 10. It stayed that way through most of the game before the Bulls climbed back into the game. The score was tied at 86 with 28 seconds left, when Michael passed the ball to Steve Kerr who made the shot that put the Bulls ahead for good. The Chicago Bulls had their fifth championship.

In June 1997 the Chicago Bulls were successful in their Strive for Five—the effort to earn their fifth NBA championship. From left to right, Dennis Rodman, Michael Jordan, Scottie Pippen, Ron Harper, and coach Phil Jackson show off their five trophies to the thousands of fans gathered to celebrate the event at Chicago's Grant Park.

⇒ ANOTHER RING, ANOTHER RETIREMENT ⇐

Before the 1997-98 season began, Michael signed a one-year contract with the Bulls for $38 million. Fans hoped for another three-peat, and the Bulls appeared quite capable of winning it all again. However, early season injuries to Pippen and Michael left the Bulls in sixth place in their division. Somehow, the Bulls pulled it together and finished the season tied with Utah for the best record in the league.

After two easy rounds and a tough seven-game series against the Indiana Pacers, the Bulls entered the finals, again facing the Utah Jazz. It was another great series between Michael Jordan and Karl Malone, but in the end the Bulls won 4-2. Defying the odds and the critics, the Chicago Bulls had posted their second "three-peat."

The victory celebration was Michael's last. Coach Phil Jackson retired. Bulls' management decided to rebuild the team. Pippen was traded to Houston, and the 1998-99 season was delayed by a lockout between owners and players that lasted until January 6, 1999.

At a January 13 press conference Michael told reporters he was retiring from basketball. After explaining that the decision had been difficult, he shared how the game had helped him accomplish his dreams:

"Ever since I was a small boy, I dreamed of playing basketball at the highest level of competition. I dreamed of playing in college and winning a national championship. I dreamed of playing in the Olympics and winning a gold medal. I dreamed of playing in the National Basketball Association and winning a world championship. Thanks to my teammates and my coaches, and to the support of many other people, these dreams have come true. I have always played basketball for the love of the game. It has never been anything more than that."

Michael Jordan takes a swing at the Michael Jordan Celebrity Invitational golf tournament held at the Ocean Club golf course, in the Bahamas. After his second retirement from basketball, in 1999, Michael decided to establish the annual fundraiser, held each January, in which celebrities compete and raise money for charitable causes. To date, the event has earned more than $4 million.

5

Wizards and the Warrior

RETIRED AGAIN, THIS TIME AT AGE 36, MICHAEL was adamant that he was going to spend his retirement doing more things in the business world, spending more time with his children and wife, Juanita, and playing more golf. To keep himself involved in basketball on some level, however, he purchased part-ownership in the Washington Wizards.

⇒ BECOMING A PRIVATE CITIZEN ⇐

In transitioning his life from pro athlete to private citizen, Michael spent a good bit of his time raising money for his various charities and being an at-home dad. He was learning how to move on in life without having an 82-game schedule filling up most of his days, nights, and weekends.

Some of the charitable efforts were as simple as a visit to a local Chicago high school in order to impress on the students the importance of a good education. On March 17, 1999, Michael visited Marshall Metro High School on Chicago's West Side. The 1,150 students there were stunned to see Jordan waiting for them in the school's auditorium. As the school's guest "Principal for a Day," Michael spoke to the students about the need for getting good grades. And he emphasized the need to have a plan or find oneself without options later in life.

Michael also found a way to combine his love of golf with raising money for charity by making plans for the first Michael Jordan Celebrity Invitational. The inaugural golf tournament was held in January 2001 on Paradise Island, Bahamas. Michael enlisted the participation of numerous celebrities, including Denver Broncos quarterback John Elway, Olympic speed skater Dan Jansen, NBA star Charles Barkley, and ice hockey great Wayne Gretzky. Proceeds from the tournament, which has been held each subsequent year, goes to a variety of charities. They include the Ronald McDonald Houses of North Carolina, the James Jordan Foundation, the Butch Kerzner Memorial Fund, and the Atlantis HIV/AIDS initiative. As of 2008, the Invitational has raised more than $4 million dollars for many causes.

⇛ WASHINGTON WIZARDS ⇚

By becoming a part-owner of the Washington Wizards, Michael was staying connected to the sport he loved, while gaining experience in the business side of pro basketball. Soon after becoming a minority owner in the Wizards, he also took on the job of director of operations. With his new front-office job, Michael became involved in many of the day-to-day activities of the team.

During the announcement of his joining the Wizards' front office, Michael talked candidly about his new duties, which included drafting, trading, and signing players, as well as hiring and firing coaches. At the January 2000 press conference he said:

> **❝This is new to me. Being in charge is something that I never had an opportunity to do. Maybe that's not the ingredient that may turn this team around. Then again, it may be. That's the beauty of trying. I won't be wearing the Wizards' uniform. I have an attitude about the way I play. I have an attitude about the way I win, and my job and responsibility with this organization is to see if I can pass it on to the players in that uniform.❞**

Michael Jordan (right) and Kerzner International official Butch Kerzner (left) present a $200,000 check to American Red Cross representative J. Logan Seitz on behalf of the Michael Jordan Celebrity Invitational. The January 2005 donation was intended for victims of the December 2004 Indian Ocean tsunami. One of the world's deadliest natural disasters, the tsunami killed more than 200,000 people.

Michael noted that he was happy to still be a part of the game he loved and to which he had devoted most of his life playing to the best of his ability. Now he would have a chance to mentor some of the younger players and share his experiences of being on the court and playing against some of the greatest players in NBA history.

⋙ BACK, BUT ONLY BRIEFLY ⋘

But Michael soon was wearing the Wizards uniform. It turned out that he couldn't stay away from playing basketball for long. On September 25, 2001, Michael made it official. He sold his interest in

Michael Jordan of the Washington Wizards passes behind his back while playing against the Philadelphia 76ers during a November 2001 game at the MCI Center in Washington, D.C. Michael played with the Wizards for just two years, before announcing his third—and final—retirement from playing NBA basketball. During his career he averaged 30.1 points per game—the most in NBA history.

the Wizards and at age 38 re-entered the world of NBA basketball. Critics thought Jordan was making a mistake, but his response was that he had missed the challenges the game presented and he missed competing against other formidable opponents in the league.

After working off his rustiness from being out of the game for a while, Michael was soon drawing huge crowds who hoped to glimpse the talents he had already demonstrated in achieving his six NBA championship titles, five NBA MVP awards, and six NBA Finals MVP awards. Jordan could still leap high and dunk hard, put up a jump shot that just swished through the net, and run the offense like a general on the court. Although the Wizards ended up with a losing season, winning only 37 games, they showed great improvement over the previous season's record of just 19 wins.

Entering the 2002-03 season, Michael was averaging 31.0 points a game. If he wasn't the Michael Jordan of the 1990s, he certainly was close. Unfortunately, he had hurt his knee in pre-season play and while it healed he no longer started for the team, and he never really got his groove back on a consistent basis. There were flashes of brilliance, like his one-handed flying dunk, or string of baskets without a miss. Overall, his play was inconsistent and he couldn't seem to play with the same ease he had throughout his career. Amid buzz about the erosion of his play, Michael announced in November 2002 that he was retiring for good at the end of the 2002-03 season.

Fans knew this was really Michael Jordan's final year in the NBA. Throughout the rest of the 2002-03 basketball season they gave him standing ovations at every arena he played in. On April 16, 2003, he was in Philadelphia making his last appearance in an NBA uniform. The Philadelphia 76ers crowd applauded and cheered as he made his last shot, which was a free throw after a foul.

When the final buzzer sounded, 40-year-old Michael Jordan had completed a career that spanned 15 seasons. He had played a total of 41,011 minutes over 1,072 games. And he had tallied a total of 32,292 points, the third best in NBA history, behind Kareem Abdul-Jabbar and Karl Malone.

⇒ LIFE AFTER BASKETBALL ⇐

Shortly after ending his basketball career Michael got involved with a new sport. He formed the Michael Jordan Motorsports AMA Superbike Team. Instead of getting a rush from dunking a basketball, he was getting his adrenaline pumped racing a motorcycle around a track. When asked by *The Cycle News* online reporter Paul Carruthers about his new sporting interest, Michael explained how he came to be involved:

> **❝Actually, I grew up riding dirt bikes and I had no ambition of getting into any kind of racing. Although I grew up watching NASCAR quite a bit, I never saw that as a business opportunity for me. I kind of got into this whole thing by mistake. I was riding on the streets one time and ran into a couple of friends and we started riding together. One of them had aspirations of riding in the AMA and . . . I thought at least I could sponsor him and give him his dream and give an opportunity to succeed. And once I got a taste of it, I was hooked.❞**

⇛ FAMILY MATTERS ⇚

For Michael, it is especially gratifying that his sons, Jeffrey and Marcus, share their dad's love of basketball. They are very competitive in their play against the legendary star who happens to be their father. And they say that Michael plays just as competitively against them in pick-up games and backyard basket shoots.

In 2007 Marcus played as a sophomore and Jeffrey as a senior for the basketball team of their high school, the Loyola Academy, located in Wilmette, Illinois. Michael regularly attended the boys' games, although because of his celebrity he sometimes found it difficult to watch them without being interrupted by fans.

Following graduation, Jeffrey Jordan enrolled at the University of Illinois, where as a freshman he has played guard for the Fighting Illini. Brother Marcus continues to play basketball for his high school team under the watchful eye of his dad.

⇛ A NEW ENDEAVOR ⇚

CROSS-CURRENTS
To learn more about another Jordan who believed putting his life at risk was just part of helping his team, read "Wearing a Different Uniform." Go to page 53. ▸▸

In 2006 Michael dipped back into the business side of the NBA, by partnering with Black Entertainment Television (BET) founder Robert L. Johnson to become part-owner of the **expansion team** the Charlotte Bobcats. Johnson, a very

Wearing a shirt with the team logo of an orange bobcat head on a blue and silver basketball, Michael Jordan talks with reporters after a December 2007 workout with the Charlotte Bobcats at their arena in Charlotte, North Carolina. After becoming a part-owner of the expansion team in June 2006, Michael took on the position of head of basketball operations.

successful African-American businessman, had the highest regard for his new, younger partner. In announcing Michael's partnership in the team, Johnson said:

    ❝Ever since I acquired the Bobcats franchise, one of my goals has been to get Michael Jordan to

become my partner in operating the team. I don't think I have to make the case for Michael's basketball expertise, his knowledge or his competitiveness as a player. I am very excited to have a native North Carolinian be a part of the Bobcats and excited to have a friend of mine—who I have absolute confidence in—oversee our basketball personnel decision making process. **"**

The team is still in its growing stages, but Michael is optimistic. In 2008 Larry Brown, the legendary NBA coach, signed on to help make the Charlotte Bobcats a successful basketball franchise.

CROSS-CURRENTS

To learn more about Michael's latest basketball team, read "The Charlotte Bobcats." Go to page 52. ▶▶

⇉ THE NEXT GREAT PLAYER ⇇

Michael Jordan has said that he believes more superstar basketball players will follow him in the future. Different greats come along in different eras. Someday, there will be another youngster with tremendous abilities who will come along and surpass the greatness of Chamberlain, Magic, Abdul-Jabbar, Shaq, Parker, and Jordan. In his autobiography *For the Love of the Game*, Michael says:

"Somewhere there is a little kid working to enhance what we've done. It may take a while, but someone will come along who approaches the game the way I did. He won't skip steps. He won't be afraid. He will learn from my example, just as I learned from others. . . . Unless they change the height of the basket or otherwise alter the dimensions of the game, there will be a player much greater than me. **"**

Notable MVPs in NBA Finals History

Michael Jordan has won more NBA Finals MVP awards than any other player in the history of the league. In each of Chicago's six NBA championships he was voted the NBA Finals MVP six times. Although no one has won as many times as Michael, other multiple NBA Finals MVPs are:

Shaquille O'Neal

The 7'1" and 325-pound basketball center with a size 22 shoe is a four-time NBA champion. While playing for the Los Angeles Lakers, he led the team to three championships and was named the NBA Finals MVP in 2000, 2001, and 2002. O'Neal has played on four NBA teams, starting his pro career with the Orlando Magic before being traded to the Lakers in 1996. Traded to the Miami Heat in the summer of 2004, O'Neal assisted in guiding the Heat on June 20, 2006, to their only NBA championship to date. In February 2008, O'Neal was traded to the Phoenix Suns.

Tim Duncan

The 6'11" and 260-pound native of St. Croix, the U.S. Virgin Islands, Duncan was a member of the 2004 U.S. Olympic team that came away with a bronze medal in Athens, Greece. He has four NBA championship rings with the San Antonio Spurs, and was named NBA Finals MVP in three of those wins. Duncan didn't begin playing organized basketball until he was in the ninth grade and has a peculiar ritual of wearing his practice shorts backwards, a habit he started as a player at Wake Forest University.

Earvin "Magic" Johnson

In one of the most memorable NCAA title games, Johnson led the Michigan State Spartans to the 1979 championship against future NBA star Larry Bird and the undefeated Indiana Hoosiers. In his rookie season with the Los Angeles Lakers, 6' 9", 250-pound Johnson played all five positions and scored 42 points in the 1980 NBA Final against the Philadelphia 76ers to earn his first of three (1980, 1982, 1987) series MVP awards. After testing positive for HIV in 1991, Johnson retired from the NBA. He did play with the 1992 United States Olympic Dream Team, winning a gold medal. In 2003, Johnson became the first Spartan inducted into the NBA Hall of Fame.

(Go back to page 9.) ◀◀

CROSS-CURRENTS

Dean Smith, UNC Men's Basketball Coach

During the course of his 36-year career as head coach of the University of North Carolina men's basketball program, Dean Smith coached the Tar Heels to more NCAA tournament game wins than any other coach in history. Born in February 1931, the Emporia, Kansas, native had been a member of a championship team himself—the 1952 NCAA champion Kansas University Jayhawks.

In 1961, 30-year-old Smith became head coach of the University of North Carolina Tar Heels. Though the team had a losing season in his first year as coach, they went on to 35 straight winning seasons. As head coach Smith compiled an unprecedented record, winning more NCAA tournament games than any other collegiate basketball coach. Under Coach Smith, the Tar Heels made 11 NCAA Final Four appearances and won two NCAA Titles (1982, 1993). When he retired in 1997 he had a record 879 wins as a head coach of NCAA Division I men's basketball.

Smith was known as an innovator and a coach who emphasized good sportsmanship. He recruited the university's first African-American scholarship player, Charlie Scott. Smith demonstrated respect for the other teams by standing on the sidelines and clapping at the beginning of games during the introductions of players from visiting teams. He introduced the tradition of starting the seniors on his teams in the final home game of the season. He explained that he remembered how he felt when as a senior basketball player at Kansas he hadn't been a starter and did not get to start in his last home game. Senior Day became a tradition at UNC that has been adopted by other colleges in the United States.

One of Smith's many accomplishments is guiding the 1976 U.S. men's basketball team to a gold medal win at the Summer Olympic Games in Montreal. Highly respected by coaches and players throughout the college ranks, Coach Smith was honored in 1982 by being inducted into the Basketball Hall of Fame. In 1997, the year of his retirement from UNC as head coach, Smith was named *Sports Illustrated* Sportsman of the Year.

In November 2006, Dean Smith was inducted into the National Collegiate Basketball Hall of Fame, a recently established organization that celebrates great basketball played on the collegiate level. Smith was honored in the inaugural class that also featured Oscar Robertson, Bill Russell, Dean Smith, John Wooden and the family of basketball founder James Naismith.

(Go back to page 14.)

Notable UNC Alumni

Michael Jordan and teammates James Worthy and Sam Perkins would go on to outstanding careers in the NBA. They are just three of the many great achievers who attended the University of North Carolina. Other UNC alumni who have gained fame include the following:

IN BUSINESS

Richard Curtis (1972): Founder, Managing Editor, *USA Today*

David Gardner (1988): Cofounder of the Motley Fool

William B. Harrison, Jr. (1966): Former chief executive officer and chairman of JP Morgan Chase

Ken Thompson (1973): Chairman and chief executive officer of Wachovia Corporation

IN ENTERTAINMENT AND BROADCASTING

Rick Dees (1972): Radio personality

Louise Fletcher (1957): Actress

Andy Griffith (1949): Actor

Charles Kuralt (1955): Journalist

IN POLITICS

Erskine Bowles (1967): Former White House Chief of Staff

John Edwards (1977, School of Law): U.S. Senator

IN SPORTS

Jim Beatty (1957): First person to run a four-minute mile on an indoor track

Garbed in a jester's hat in honor of his company, the Motley Fool, UNC graduate David Gardner addresses a 2004 conference in Atlanta, Georgia. Gardner graduated in 1988 from the University of North Carolina at Chapel Hill. Later, he and his brother Tom David founded the Motley Fool, a newsletter and Web site that features stock market and investment advice.

Mia Hamm (1994): Soccer player; member of the U.S. Women's National Team

Davis Love III (1986): Professional golfer

Lawrence Taylor (1981): Professional football player; Football Hall of Famer

(Go back to page 17.)

NBA Rookies of the Year

In October 1996, as part of the 50th anniversary celebration of the National Basketball Association (NBA), Commissioner David Stern announced the names of the 50 Greatest Players in NBA history. These 50 extraordinary basketball players had been selected by members of the media, former players and coaches, current and former general managers, and team executives. Of the 50 players chosen, 17 had also been Rookie of the Year winners.

The first Rookie of the Year Eddie Gottlieb trophy was presented to Milwaukee Hawks forward Bob Pettit in 1953. Michael Jordan was honored with the Eddie Gottlieb trophy in 1985. The two basketball players are part of an elite group that includes 15 other players who have received both Rookie of the Year honors and the distinction of having been named one of the 50 Greatest Players in NBA history.

Those other players are:
• Elgin Baylor, Minneapolis Lakers (1959)
• Wilt Chamberlain, Philadelphia Warriors (1960)
• Oscar Roberson, Cincinnati Royals (1961)
• Jerry Lucas, Cincinnati Royals (1964)
• Willis Reed, New York Knicks (1965)
• Rick Barry, San Francisco Warriors (1966)
• Dave Bing, Detroit Pistons (1967)
• Earl Monroe, Baltimore Bullets (1968)
• Wes Unseld, Baltimore Bullets (1969)
• Kareem Abdul-Jabbar, Milwaukee Bucks (1970)
• Dave Cowens, Boston Celtics (1971)
• Larry Bird, Boston Celtics (1980)
• Patrick Ewing, New York Knicks (1986)
• David Robinson, San Antonio Spurs (1990)
• Shaquille O'Neal, Orlando Magic (1993)

(Go back to page 20.)

Pro Athletes Who Play Other Sports

Michael Jordan's decision to try to play professional baseball after being one of the most dominant basketball players to ever step onto the hardwood court was unusual. However, it was not the first time a successful pro athlete participated in more than one sport.

One actor actually began his career as a sports pro. Chuck Connors, who became known for his television role as Lucas McCain on *The Rifleman* (1958-63) played a couple of sports before becoming an actor. He played pro basketball for the Boston Celtics and then switched to baseball. It was while he was playing for the Los Angeles Angels that he was

spotted by an MGM casting director. Connors was given a small part in the film *Pat and Mike* (1952). He enjoyed performing, and after critics praised his performance in *The Big Country* (1958) Connors gave up baseball to develop his acting career.

Olympic pentathlon and decathlon competitor Jim Thorpe has often been regarded as the greatest athlete of the 20th century. In addition to winning Olympic gold medals at the 1912 Games, held in Stockholm, Sweden, Thorpe was a successful professional baseball and football player. He played baseball for six years with professional baseball teams before moving on to play football for another eight years. Thorpe was a charter inductee in the Pro Football Hall of Fame in 1963 and was named to the Track and Field Hall of Fame in 1975.

Two NFL football stars, Bo Jackson and Deion Sanders, also had successful careers on the baseball diamond. Jackson never won a championship, but he was the first athlete selected to play in the All-Star Games of two major sports. He played on three MLB teams and was an explosive running back for the Los Angeles Raiders. Deion Sanders was a force in pro football and baseball. He is the only player to have appeared in both a World Series (Atlanta Braves) and two Super Bowls (San Francisco and Dallas). Sanders was also the first football pro in 34 years to play both offense and defense in the same game.

Joining Michael Jordan with a double sports career in basketball and baseball was New York Knicks great Dave DeBusschere. Upon graduation from the University of Detroit in 1962, DeBusschere signed contracts with both the Chicago White Sox and the Detroit Pistons. Ultimately DeBusschere was a standout in basketball, and was voted one of the 50 Greatest Players in NBA history.

Deion Sanders of San Francisco 49ers. He played both football and baseball in college, at Florida State University, in Tallahassee. He then went on to successful careers in both sports, playing 14 years for five different National Football League teams and 9 years for four Major League Baseball teams.

(Go back to page 30.) ◀◀

Jordan's Brief Baseball Career

Although he was never called up to play for the Chicago White Sox major league team, Michael did post respectable statistics during his minor league play. While playing with the AA minor league Birmingham Barons, Michael demonstrated better defensive than hitting abilities. Playing right field, he had the speed that enabled him to run down fly balls. He was also a great base stealer, when he was able to get a hit.

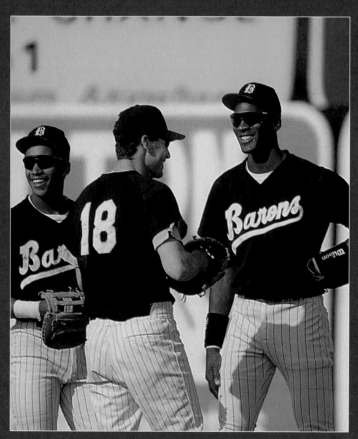

Michael Jordan (right) of the Birmingham Barons talks with team-mates during practice. A member of the Southern League, the AA affiliate of the Chicago White Sox plays its home games at Regions Park, in Hoover, Alabama, outside the city of Birmingham. During Jordan's one full season in the minors, he struck out 114 times and made 11 errors.

On April 8, 1994, Jordan played his first professional baseball game. After a 0 for 3 start at the plate, he went on a 13-game hitting streak and was batting .378. In subsequent games, however, Jordan did not hit consistently, and by the end of July was hitting under .200. Then, on July 30 he hit his first home run and in the same game knocked out a double. He ended his first season in the minors batting .202, 3 home runs, 51 runs batted in, and 30 stolen bases.

Although determined to give baseball his best effort, Jordan found that his attempt to break into the sport came at the worst time. In the fall of 1994, the Major League Baseball season ended before its championship contest—the World Series—took place. Unable to reach a salary agreement with the team owners, MLB players went on strike that October.

From the start of the strike, Michael made it clear that he had no intention of crossing the picket lines of other players on strike. And he said he would not attend spring training games because his presence might draw fans while the strike was still underway.

Because of his attempt to fulfill a dream by playing professional baseball, Michael developed the utmost respect for the minor leagues. He explained:

> **"I met thousands of new fans, and I learned that minor league players are really the foundation of baseball. They often play in obscurity and with little recognition, but they deserve the respect of the fans and everyone associated with the game."**

(Go back to page 32.)

Wearing a Different Uniform

James Jordan, Jr., Michael Jordan's oldest brother, shares many of the same traits as his superstar brother. Like Michael, James conveys a sense of self-confidence and has a clean-shaven head. In his line of work, he also wears a uniform. James does not play a pro sport, however. His uniform is the one he wears as a soldier in the United States Army.

James, too, is a part of a team. And in November 2004, even though he was eligible to retire after 30 years of service, Commander Sergeant Major Jordan announced he was extending his Army service by another year.

His brigade, the 35th Signal Brigade, was being deployed to Iraq, and James said that he wanted to be with the 500 other members of his brigade who had received orders to head overseas.

After returning from Iraq, James retired in April 2006. Michael was present at his older brother's retirement ceremony, held at Fort Bragg, North Carolina, but the focus of those in attendance was not on the basketball celebrity. It was clearly on honoring James for his 31 years of service in the Army.

(Go back to page 44.)

The Charlotte Bobcats

Since 1988 the city of Charlotte, North Carolina, had its own basketball team, the Charlotte Hornets. Then, before the start of the 2002-03 NBA season, the team moved to New Orleans. The NBA promised the city an expansion team. The franchise for the new team was awarded to Black Entertainment Television founder Robert L. Johnson. He became one of the first African-American owners of an American sports team.

The team held a contest to come up with an appropriate name. The organization eventually settled on the name *Bobcats*, since the bobcat is one of the few native wild cats in North Carolina. "Bob" is also a nickname for Robert (a reference to owner Robert L. Johnson). By 2005 the Charlotte Bobcats Arena was built.

The next step was to assemble the players on the team. Through the 2004 NBA draft and some trading, the Bobcats acquired Emeka Okafor, a former University of Connecticut forward who helped the Huskies win the NCAA championship. He had been named the NCAA Basketball Tournament Most Outstanding Player. In his first season with the Bobcats, Emeka Okafor was named NBA Rookie of the Year, in 2005.

In June 2006, Michael Jordan joined Johnson as part-owner of the new team. He also assumed the job of director of basketball operations. Jordan and the other members of upper management hope to improve the team, which had not posted a winning season as of 2008.

In April 2008 Larry Brown, who has 23 years of coaching experience and is the fifth-winningest coach in NBA history, was hired as the Charlotte Bobcats new head coach. He is the only head coach to ever win an NCAA championship (University of Kansas) and an NBA title (Detroit Pistons).

(Go back to page 46.)

A photograph of the Charlotte Bobcats' home court, which in 2008 was renamed the Time Warner Cable Arena. The TWC arena hosted its first Charlotte Bobcats game on November 5, 2005. The site is also home to the Charlotte Checkers, a minor league hockey team, and it serves as a venue for college basketball games and NCAA tournament games.

1963   Michael Jeffrey Jordan is born on February 17 to James and Deloris Jordan.

1982   As a University of North Carolina freshman, Jordan scores the game-winning basket on March 29 in NCAA championship game between the UNC Tar Heels and the Georgetown Hoyas.

1984   Jordan wins the gold medal as a member of the U.S. men's basketball team at the Los Angeles Summer Olympics.

Jordan is selected third in the NBA draft by the Chicago Bulls.

1985   Jordan is named NBA Rookie of the Year.

1991   Jordan leads the Chicago Bulls to their first NBA championship.

1992   Jordan wins a second gold medal as a member of the Dream Team at the Summer Olympics in Barcelona, Spain.

1993   Michael's father, James Jordan, is murdered on July 23.

On October 6, Jordan announces his retirement from the NBA.

In November Jordan signs with the Chicago White Sox to play baseball.

1995   On March 25, Jordan returns to playing professional basketball with the Chicago Bulls.

1996   Jordan leads the Bulls to a fourth NBA championship. He becomes the second player in NBA history to be named MVP of both the regular season and the playoffs, as well as MVP of the All-Star Game.

1998   The Chicago Bulls record their second "three-peat," after winning the NBA championship title for a third time in a row in June 1998. Jordan makes the game winning shot in what is his last as a Chicago Bull against the Utah Jazz to clinch the team's sixth championship.

Jordan is selected as one of the "50 Greatest Players in NBA History."

1999   On January 13, Jordan announces that he is retiring again from basketball.

2000   Jordan invests in part-ownership of the NBA Washington Wizards.

2001   The inaugural Michael Jordan Celebrity Invitational, a golf tournament and charity fundraising event, is held in January.

Jordan sells his share of ownership in the Washington Wizards, and on September 25 announces that he is coming out of retirement to play for the team.

2003   Jordan announces his third retirement from basketball. On April 16 Jordan plays his last NBA game, when the Wizards lose to the Philadelphia 76ers.

Jordan forms the Michael Jordan Motorsports AMA Superbike Team.

2006   As a result of entering into a business venture with Black Entertainment Television founder Robert L. Johnson, Jordan becomes part-owner of the NBA Charlotte Bobcats.

2008   The Charlotte Bobcats hire Larry Brown as new head coach.

Accomplishments & Awards

Six-time NBA champion (1991-93, 1996-98)
Six-time NBA Finals MVP (1991-93, 1996-98)
Five-time NBA MVP (1988, 1991, 1992, 1996, 1998)
Ten-time All-NBA First Team (1987-93, 1996-98)
Nine-time NBA All-Defensive First Team (1988-93, 1996-98)
Fourteen-time All-Star Game selection
Three-time NBA All-Star Game MVP (1988, 1996, 1998)
One of 50 Greatest Players in NBA History (1996)
Two-time Olympic gold medalist (1984, 1992).
Defensive Player of the Year (1988)
All-NBA Second Team (1985)
NBA Rookie of the Year (1985)
University NCAA championship title (1982)

Career Records:

Most consecutive games scoring 10 or more points: 866
Most free throws made, playoffs: 1,463
Most points, NBA playoffs: 5,987
Highest points-per-game average: 33.4 points per game

Career Averages

Year	Team	G	GS	MPG	FG%	3P%	FT%	STL	BLK	TO	PF	OFF	DEF	TOT	AST	PTS
84-85	CHI	82	N/A	38.3	.515	.173	.845	2.4	0.8	3.5	3.5	2.0	4.5	6.5	5.9	28.2
85-86	CHI	18	N/A	25.1	.457	.167	.840	2.1	1.2	2.5	2.6	1.3	2.3	3.6	2.9	22.7
86-87	CHI	82	N/A	40.0	.482	.182	.857	2.9	1.5	3.3	2.9	2.0	3.2	5.2	4.6	37.1
87-88	CHI	82	N/A	40.4	.535	.132	.841	3.2	1.6	3.1	3.3	1.7	3.8	5.5	5.9	35.0
88-89	CHI	81	N/A	40.2	.538	.276	.850	2.9	0.8	3.6	3.0	1.8	6.2	8.0	8.0	32.5
89-90	CHI	82	N/A	39.0	.526	.376	.848	2.8	0.7	3.0	2.9	1.7	5.2	6.8	6.3	33.6
90-91	CHI	82	N/A	37.0	.539	.312	.851	2.7	1.0	2.5	2.8	1.4	4.6	6.0	5.5	31.5
91-92	CHI	80	N/A	38.8	.519	.270	.832	2.3	0.9	2.5	2.5	1.1	5.3	6.4	6.1	30.1
92-93	CHI	78	78	39.3	.495	.352	.837	2.8	0.8	2.7	2.4	1.7	5.0	6.7	5.5	32.6
94-95	CHI	17	17	39.3	.411	.500	.801	1.8	0.8	2.1	2.8	1.5	5.4	6.9	5.3	26.9
95-96	CHI	82	82	37.7	.495	.427	.834	2.2	0.5	2.4	2.4	1.8	4.8	6.6	4.3	30.4
96-97	CHI	82	82	37.9	.486	.374	.833	1.7	0.5	2.0	1.9	1.4	4.5	5.9	4.3	29.6
97-98	CHI	82	82	38.8	.465	.238	.784	1.7	0.5	2.3	1.8	1.6	4.2	5.8	3.5	28.7
01-02	WAS	60	53	34.9	.416	.189	.790	1.4	0.4	2.7	2.0	0.8	4.8	5.6	5.2	22.9
02-03	WAS	82	67	37.0	.445	.291	.821	1.5	0.5	2.1	2.1	0.9	5.2	6.1	3.8	20.0
		G	GS	MPG	FG%	3P%	FT%	STL	BLK	TO	PF	OFF	DEF	TOT	AST	PTS
Totals		1072	461+	38.3	.497	.327	.835	2.3	0.8	2.7	2.6	1.6	4.7	6.2	5.3	30.1

Books

Jordan, Michael. *For the Love of the Game*. New York: Crown Publishers, 1998.

McCormick, Lisa Wade. *Michael Jordan*. New York: Children's Press, 2007.

McGovern, Mike. *Michael Jordan: Basketball Player*. New York: Ferguson, 2005.

Miller, Raymond. *Michael Jordan*. San Diego: Thomson Gale, 2003.

Web Sites

http://www.nba.com/playerfile/michael_jordan/index.html

National Basketball Association's official biography of Michael Jordan includes statistics on his career averages, career totals, and season and career highs.

http://www.basketball-reference.com/teams/CHI/

This comprehensive Web site provides a collection of information about the Chicago Bulls and statistics on all its past and present players.

http://www.mjcigolf.com/

This Web site features information about the Michael Jordan Celebrity Invitational, an annual golf tournament that raises funds for various charities.

http://www.jamesjordanfoundation.com/

Named in honor of Michael Jordan's father, the James R. Jordan Foundation works to help strengthen families. The organization develops and implements initiatives to help families and children, particularly in the areas of health and education.

http://www.mjflightschool.com/

Michael Jordan Flight Schools are basketball camps where youths and adults can learn fundamentals of basketball.

All-Star Game—in NBA basketball, a championship game matching the best players in the Eastern Conference against the best players in the Western Conference.

assist—the basketball statistic that records how many times the player passes the ball to another right before the second player scores a basket.

draft—in sports, the annual process by which teams select new players from the college or amateur ranks.

Dream Team—nickname for a team made up of exceptional professional players. The original U.S. men's basketball Dream Team consisted of 12 NBA stars, including Michael Jordan, Magic Johnson, and Larry Bird. The players dominated at the 1992 Olympics, held in Barcelona, Spain.

expansion team—a new team added to an established professional sports league.

franchise—a team in a professional sports league.

MVP—Most Valuable Player; an award given to a player for exceptional performances during a season, game, or playoff series. The winner of the MVP award for the NBA season receives the Maurice Podoloff Trophy.

NCAA—National Collegiate Athletic Association.

playoffs—series of games played following the regular season in which the best teams compete against each other in order to determine a league champion.

rebound—the act of gaining possession of the basketball following a failed attempted shot, either by a teammate (offensive rebound) or by an opponent (defensive rebound).

rookie—a professional athlete who is playing his or her first full season.

steals—a statistic that records the number of times that a player legally takes possession of the basketball from an opponent.

three-peat—winning three championships in a row; a combination of the words *three* and *repeat*

triple-double—an instance in which a basketball player records 10 or more in three of five categories (points, assists, rebound, blocks, or steals) in a single game.

page 6 "The Bulls knew . . ." Michael Jordan. *For the Love of the Game: My Story*. New York: Crown Publishers, 1998, p. 105.

page 6 "After all these years . . ." Michael Jordan. *For the Love of the Game*, p. 105.

page 9 "It was like I was . . ." Michael Jordan. *For the Love of the Game*, p. 108.

page 12 "My favorite childhood memory . . ." Jim Naughton. *Taking to the Air: The Rise of Michael Jordan*. New York: Warner Books, Inc., 1992, p. 44.

page 12 "He always, I think was a little . . ." Lynn Norment. "Michael's Mom: 'We Didn't Set Out to Raise a Superstar.'" *Ebony*, May 1997.

page 14 "It was embarrassing not . . ." Larry Schwartz. "Michael Jordan Transcends Hoops," ESPN.com, 2007. http://espn.go.com/sportscentury/features/00016048.html

page 20 "Even at this stage of his . . ." David Halberstam. *Playing for Keeps: Michael Jordan and the World He Made*. New York: Broadway Books, 2000. p. 156.

page 24 "I'm envious of the Detroit Pistons . . ." Clifton Brown. "Basketball: Amid Pressing Matters, Jordan Accepts M.V.P." New York Times, May 21, 1991.

page 27 "Dad is no longer . . ." "James Jordan: Shock and Sadness Follow Shooting of Michael Jordan's Father." *Jet*, August 30, 1993.

page 30 "For the last nine . . ." Ira Berkow. "A Humbled Jordan Learns New Truths," *New York Times*, April 11, 1994.

page 37 "Ever since I was a small . . ." Michael Jordan's statement. NBA Media Ventures, LLC. NBA.com, http://www.nba.com/jordan/jordanstatement.html

page 40 "This is new to me . . ." Steve Wyche. "Jordan Joins Wizards' Front Office," *The Washington Post*, January 20, 2000; Page A1.

page 44 "Actually, I grew up riding . . ." Paul Carruthers. "Michael Jordan Speaks Out." *Cycle News Online*, June 26, 2007.

page 45 "Ever since I acquired . . ." "Jordan Becomes Part-Owner of Bobcats," ESPN.com, June 16, 2006. http://sports.espn.go.com/nba/news/story?id=2486172

page 46 "Somewhere there is . . ." Michael Jordan. *For the Love of the Game*, p. 111.

page 53 "I met thousands . . ." David Kindred. "Baseball Struck Out: Michael Jordan Leaves the Chicago White Sox Organization." *The Sporting News*, March 20, 1995. http://findarticles.com/p/articles/mi_m1208/is_n12_v219/ai_16675107/pg_1

Numbers in **bold italics** refer to captions.

Judy L. Hasday, a native of Philadelphia, Pennsylvania, is a two-time graduate of Temple University, with a B.A. in Communications and an M.Ed in Educational Media. Ms. Hasday has worked as a photo editor and freelance writer for more than 25 years. She is a published author of young adult non-fiction and has more than 25 books in print. She has won five book awards including three "Best Books for Teens" from The New York Public Library, a National Social Studies Council Book Award, and one from VOYA (Voice of Youth Advocacy).

Many of Hasday's photographs have been published in books and magazines. She devotes much of her free time volunteering as a photographer for the Greater Delaware Valley Chapter of the Multiple Sclerosis Society and the Philadelphia Chapter of the National Ovarian Cancer Coalition.

PICTURE CREDITS

page

1: Nike/NMI

4: Jim Prisching/Chicago Tribune/KRT

7: Chicago Bulls Archives/SPCS

8: Chuck Berman/Chicago Tribune/KRT

10: ASP Library

13: EALHS/SPCS

15: Sports Illustrated/NMI

16: ASP Library

18: Upper Deck Co./PRMS

21: NBAE/SPCS

23: NBAE/SPCS

25: Sports Illustrated/SPCS

26: NBAE/SPCS

28: Sara Lee Branded Apparel/PRMS

31: Chicago Tribune/KRT

33: AFP Photos

34: NBAE/SPCS

36: Jose More/Chicago Tribune/KRT

38: Kerzner Int'l/NMI

41: Kerzner Int'l/NMI

42: Nathaniel S. Butler/NBAE/SPCS

45: Ken Smith/NBAE/Getty Images

49: APWA/PRMS

51: NFL/SPCS

52: SportsChrome Pix

55: A.F. Silva/T&T/IOA Photos

Front cover: NBAE/SPCS